NOAH'S ARK

Written by Timothy Knapman

Illustrated by Sean Sims

Long, long ago, a man named Noah
lived with his family.

They were good and kind people who loved all of God's creatures.

One night, God came to Noah and said, "I am going to send a flood that will cover the Earth in water. Will you take care of the animals?"

"Of course," replied Noah, "but how?"

"You must build the biggest boat there has ever been, with enough room for two of every kind of creature. You shall call it the Ark."

So Noah and his family built an Ark with rooms for all the animals. As the Ark took shape, the animals told Noah what they would need.

"A window to look out of," said the giraffes.

"A long deck where we can exercise," said the lions.

"Plenty of yummy food!" said the zebras.

"And somewhere comfy to sit and chat," said the sheep and goats.

After weeks of work, the Ark was ready, and not a moment too soon. Storm clouds were gathering and rain was on its way! "All aboard!" said Noah.

And so the animals went in two by two.

The elephants came trumpeting.

The camels came plodding.

The monkeys came laughing
as they turned somersaults.

And the rabbits came hopping in.

The animals were excited to be onboard.

The giraffes peered out of their windows.

The lions ran races on the upper deck.

And down in the cabins, the sheep
and goats settled in for a lovely chat.

The rain came down
fast and hard, and soon
the Ark was afloat!

It rained until water covered even the tallest mountains.

On board the Ark, the animals made friends.

The tigers and the lions held roaring competitions while the giraffes let the monkeys slide down their long necks.

The pandas played cards with the kangaroos,

and the elephants said hello to the penguins that swam alongside.

The bears took a stroll along the deck. All kinds of birds perched on the Ark to rest their wings.

And down below, the goats and sheep were snuggled and warm.

But day after day, night after night, the rain kept falling, and eventually the animals grew homesick.

The monkeys missed leaping through the trees.

The lions missed playing in the tall grass.

The horses missed running in the meadows.
All of them wondered, "Will this rain ever stop?"

Then, after 40 days and 40 nights,

Noah's wife said "Listen!"

It was suddenly very quiet.

"The rain has stopped at last!" cried Noah.

Outside, the sun was shining!

Slowly the water went down, and soon the animals on deck could see the tops of the tallest mountains again.

"I will send a dove to look for dry land," said Noah.

Everyone waited for the bird to return.

They waited.

And waited.

Finally the dove returned with a twig from an olive tree in its beak.
"If the dove found a tree, there must be dry land nearby," said Noah.

Sure enough, the dove showed them the way.

Noah thanked God
for saving their lives.

As a sign that he would
never flood the Earth again,
God put a rainbow in the sky.

Noah opened the doors of the Ark and
the animals went out into the world.
They couldn't wait to start a new adventure!

BUILD YOUR ARK

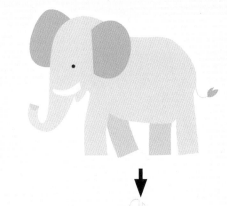

3 Push out all the character and animal pieces.

4 Slot the characters and animals into the half-circle bases to stand them up.

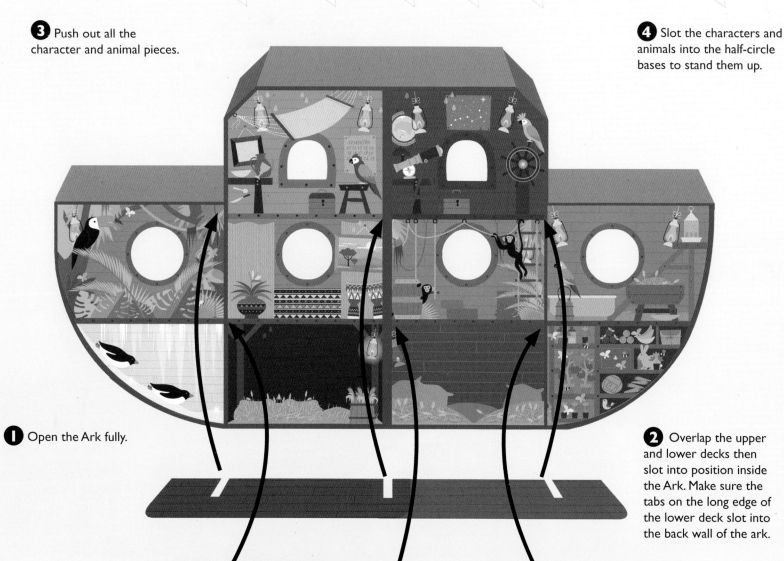

1 Open the Ark fully.

2 Overlap the upper and lower decks then slot into position inside the Ark. Make sure the tabs on the long edge of the lower deck slot into the back wall of the ark.

Silver Dolphin Books
An imprint of Printers Row Publishing Group
10350 Barnes Canyon Road, Suite 100, San Diego, CA 92121
www.silverdolphinbooks.com

Copyright © 2016 Quarto Children's Books Ltd

Written by Timothy Knapman
Illustrated by Sean Sims
Paper engineering by Jayne Evans

Printers Row Publishing Group is a division of Readerlink Distribution Services, LLC.
Silver Dolphin Books is a registered trademark of Readerlink Distribution Services, LLC.

All notations of errors or omissions should be addressed to Silver Dolphin Books, Editorial
Department, at the above address. All other correspondence (author inquiries, permissions)
concerning the content of this book should be addressed to Quarto Children's Books Ltd,
The Old Brewery, 6 Blundell Street, London N7 9BH UK.

ISBN: 978-1-62686-839-7

Manufactured, printed, and assembled in Shenzhen, China.
20 19 18 17 16 1 2 3 4 5